...I NEVER THOUGHT I WOULD AGAIN...

IN LOVING MEMORY

OF FRANK MATHESON

15th MARCH 1932

-

23RD SEPTEMBER 2017

WRITTEN BY

COLIN BOYNTON

ISBN: 978-0-9559931-8-3

INDEX

1. !!!!!

IT'S SO SAD AND TRUE
BUT THERE'S THINGS THAT WE'LL DO
THAT WILL BREAK, EACH OTHERS HEART
NOT JUST YOU AND ME
BUT THE STRANGERS WE SEE
WHO ARE TEARING OUR LIVES APART.

CAUSING YOU PAIN
TIME AND AGAIN
BRINGING US TERRORS AND FEARS
FOR OUR TOMORROWS
THEY'RE BRINGING US SORROWS
AND EYES THAT ARE BLINDED BY TEARS.

WITH LOVE IN OUR HEART
THAT WE'RE TEARING APART
WHAT IS IT ALL LEADING TO
SET YOUR LOVE FREE
AND LET THE WORLD SEE
THERE'S SOME THINGS WE JUST SHOULDN'T DO

2. THIS WORLD

STOP WHAT YOU'RE DOING
TAKE A LOOK AROUND
THIS WORLD IT IS SO BEAUTIFUL
FROM SKY DOWN TO THE GROUND
THE HILLS AND THE DALES
THE FORESTS AND THE TREES
FROM THE HIGHEST MOUNTAINS
DOWN TO THE DEEPEST SEAS
THE COLOURS OF THE RAINBOW
IN EVERY SHADE AND HUE
FROM DARKEST SKIES AT MIDNIGHT
TO SUNNY SKIES OF BLUE
BIRDS THAT SING SO SWEETLY
AND BEASTS DOWN ON THE GROUND
THE LOUDEST ROAR IN AFRICA
TO THE FAINTEST SOUND
THE FLOWERS IN A GARDEN
AND HEDGEROW FLOWERS TOO
BLOSSOM ON THE TREE TOPS
ALL LOOK FRESH AND NEW
EACH THING IN ITS OWN WAY
SO BEAUTIFUL AND FREE
PAUSE A WHILE AND LOOK AROUND
AND SEE THE THINGS I SEE.

3. JUST A FANTASY ?

SING A SONG OF HAPPINESS
WHERE EVERYTHING IS WELL
WITH PEACE AND LOVE ACROSS THE LAND
AND NOTHING MORE TO TELL
WALKING HAND IN HAND IN HAND
NO HATRED AND NO FEAR
EVERYBODY WEARS A SMILE
AND NO ONE SHEDS A TEAR
WHERE EVERYBODY GETS ALONG
AND EVERYONE'S YOUR FRIEND
NO ONE HURTS EACH OTHER
NO BROKEN HEARTS TO MEND
A WORLD THAT'S FREE FROM POVERTY
NO HUNGER AND NO THIRST
NO LONGER ARE WE SELFISH
WE PUT THE OTHERS FIRST
WITH NO MORE GUNS AND NO MORE BOMBS
AND NO ONE GETTING MAIMED
IS THIS JUST A FANTASY ?
AND SHOULD WE FEEL ASHAMED ?

4. BEST FRIENDS

HIDDEN IN A CUPBOARD
YOU STEPPED OUT OF MY MIND
SHOULD I TELL SOMEBODY
OR WOULD THAT BE UNKIND
YOU SAID THAT YOU HAD BEEN AROUND
FOR SUCH A LONG TIME NOW
I DON'T KNOW WHERE YOU CAME FROM
OR EVEN WHEN OR HOW
SOME PEOPLE THINK I'M CRAZY
WHEN THEY HEAR ME SPEAK
WITH NO ONE STOOD BESIDE ME
THEY THINK MY MIND IS WEAK
THEY DO NOT SEE WHAT I SEE
OR HEAR THE THINGS I DO
HAVE THEY GOT A FRIEND LIKE ME
OR GOT A FRIEND LIKE YOU
SO AM I GOING CRAZY
OR AM I GOING MAD
OR IS MY "FRIEND" THE BEST FRIEND
A PERSON EVER HAD
NEVER ANSWERS BACK TO ME
LISTENS WHAT I SAY
AND ALWAYS READY WAITING
BE IT NIGHT OR DAY
IMAGINARY BEST FRIEND
YOU'RE NEVER FAR AWAY
YOU'VE BEEN WITH ME FOREVER
I HOPE IT STAYS THAT WAY
IMAGNARY BEST FRIEND
OR ONLY IN MY MIND
I'VE HAD HIM SINCE MY CHILDHOOD
HE'S LOYAL, TRUE AND KIND

5. CAN THIS BE TRUE ?

IS THERE ANY WONDER
THE WORLD IS IN A MESS
INSTEAD OF PREACHING LOVE
WE'RE TEACHING HATREDNESS
WITH TERROR EVER GROWING
WHILE PEOPLE LIVE IN FEAR
HURTFUL THINGS AND SPITEFUL THINGS
ARE ALL I EVER HEAR
WE DO NOT PULL TOGETHER
WHY CAN'T WE JUST AGREE
WE'RE BUILDING WALLS AROUND US
SOON NO ONE WILL BE FREE
WE ONLY HAVE ONE LIFE TO LIVE
AND WHAT WE LEAVE BEHIND
WILL BE A LASTING LEGACY
WE'RE GIVING TO MANKIND

6. WORLD WAR GONE

AFTER THE FIGHTING
AND AFTER THE WAR
WE NEVER FOUND PEACE
THAT OUR SOLDIERS DIED FOR
THEY FOUGHT FOR DEMOCRACY
DIED FOR OUR RIGHTS
DIED WITH THE HOPE
WE'D SLEEP SAFELY AT NIGHTS
THEY BRAVELY FOUGHT ON
THROUGH BAD DAYS AND GOOD
ON SEAS AND IN TRENCHES
IN SUNSHINE AND MUD
HOW SOON WE FORGOT
WHAT OUR BRAVE MEN DIED FOR
WE KEEP GOING BACKWARDS
AND FIGHTING SOME MORE
THE MORE THAT WE FIGHT
THE MORE SOULS ARE GONE
AND MORE HEARTS ARE BROKEN
WE JUST CARRY ON
AND AFTER THE FIGHTING
WE ASK "WHAT'S IT FOR?"
WE JUST KEEP ON MARCHING
TO YET ONE MORE WAR!

7. INVISIBLE MAN

I SEE A LOT OF FACES
ALMOST EVERY DAY
ALL OF THEM ARE DIFFERENT
AND GOING ON THEIR WAY
VERY FEW WILL SMILE AT YOU
AND EVEN LESS WILL SPEAK
AM I JUST INVISIBLE
IT HAPPENS EVERY WEEK.

I SEE THE SAME OLD FACES
EACH AND EVERY DAY
I DON'T KNOW THEM, THEY DON'T KNOW ME
AND PASS ALONG THE WAY
NO ONE WANTS TO LOOK AT YOU
THEY TURN TO FACE THE FLOOR
AM I JUST INVISIBLE
OR IS THERE SOMETHING MORE

I SEE THE DIFFERENT FACES
PASSING EVERY DAY
WHY NOT SMILE AND SAY HELLO
THEN CARRY ON YOUR WAY
IT WOULDN'T HURT NOBODY
AND ISN'T HARD TO DO
FOR I AM NOT INVISIBLE
I'M JUST THE SAME AS YOU.

8. PEACE ON EARTH

NOTHING STIRRED AND NOTHING MOVED
NOTHING MADE A SOUND
EVEN NATURE'S CREATURES
LAY LOW UPON THE GROUND
AND EVEN THOUGH THE DAYLIGHT
HAD STARTED LONG AGO
YOU'D SWEAR THAT IF YOU LISTENED
YOU'D HEAR THE FLOWERS GROW
ACROSS THE LAND ALL WAS STILL
NOT A SINGLE BREEZE
NOTHING STIRRED THE BRANCHES
OR LEAVES UPON THE TREES
NO ONE LEFT THEIR HOUSES
EVERYONE STAYED HOME
EVEN LITTLE CREATURES
STAYED SNUGGLED UP AND WARM
STILL NOTHING MOVED AND NOTHING STIRRED
OR MADE THE SLIGHTEST SOUND
ALL BECAUSE THE WORLD ABOUT
HAD NOW BECOME FOG BOUND

9. THE GOOD OLD DAYS

IN GOOD OLD DAYS WHEN GRASS WAS GREEN
THE SUN SHONE WAY UP HIGH
BIRDS SANG IN THE TREETOPS
OR FLEW ACROSS THE SKY
FLOWERS GREW SO BRIGHT AND GAY
OUT THERE IN THE WILD
THE GOOD OLD DAYS SEEMED BETTER THEN
WHEN I WAS JUST A CHILD

IN GOOD OLD DAYS WHEN SKIES WERE BLUE
AND CLOUDS WENT SLOWLY BY
BIRDS AND BEES WERE ALL AROUND
AS WELL AS BUTTERFLY
LIVING HAD A SLOWER PACE
WE MOVED IN DIFFERENT WAYS
HAVE THINGS REALLY CHANGED THAT MUCH
FROM THE GOOD OLD DAYS

IN GOOD OLD DAYS WHEN STARS WOULD SHINE
IN THE DARK NIGHT SKY
A BREEZE SEEMED MUCH MORE GENTLE THEN
AS IT WENT ON BY
PERHAPS WE JUST DON'T NOTICE
RUSHING ON OUR WAYS
THAT THINGS ARE NOT THAT DIFFERENT
FROM THE GOOD OLD DAYS.

10.A NEW DAY DAWNS

I KNOW A NEW DAY'S STARTING
FOR I HEAR THE BIRDS ARE SINGING
I LISTEN TO THE SOUND THEY MAKE
AND HEAR THE JOY THEY'RE BRINGING
THE SUN WILL RISE UP IN THE SKY
BRINGING WARMTH AND LIGHT
ENDING ALL THE COLD AND DARK
THAT FILLS THE LONGEST NIGHT
AND SLOWLY NOW THE WORLD AWAKES
INTO A BRAND NEW DAY
FILLED WITH THINGS OF BEAUTY
IN EVERY LITTLE WAY

11. GOING ROUND

LET'S GO ROUND AGAIN
RELIVE SOME HAPPY DAYS
BRINGING BACK SOME MEMORIES
IN VERY DIFFERENT WAYS
LOOKING AT OLD PHOTOGRAPHS
OR FLICKING THROUGH A BOOK
BRINGING BACK SOME MEMORIES
WITH JUST A SINGLE LOOK
RELIVING THINGS WE DID TOGETHER
PLACES WE WENT TO
BRINGING BACK SOME MEMORIES
OF TIMES THAT WE ONCE KNEW
REMINDING US OF PEOPLE
SOME OF THEM LONG GONE
AND ALL OF THESE OLD MEMORIES
WILL JUST KEEP LIVING ON.

12. PARTING OF THE WAYS

BROKEN DREAMS AND PROMISES
A POCKET FULL OF LIES
HURTFUL WORDS WERE SPOKEN
UNDER STARLIT SKIES
TEARS FELL LIKE RAINDROPS
DOWN A SADDENED FACE
BACKS WERE TURNED TO WALK AWAY
AND LEAVE A CERTAIN PLACE
NOT QUITE FEELING BITTER
NOT QUITE FEELING BLUE
BUT PARTING BROUGHT SUCH SORROW
BETWEEN THE PARTING TWO
AND AS THEY PARTED COMPANY
TO GO THEIR SEPERATE WAY
THEY TURNED TO FACE EACH OTHER
BOTH ABOUT TO SAY
THEY SMILED AT ONE ANOTHER
SO CHEERFUL AND SO BRIGHT
THIS PARTING WAS SO WRONG FOR THEM
THEY HELD EACH OTHER TIGHT.

13. NEVER A KNIGHT OR PRINCE.

I MAY NOT BE A DASHING PRINCE,
OR KNIGHT UPON A STEED,
I MAY NOT BE A HERO
TO SAVE US WHEN WE NEED.
ALL I AM IS WHO I AM,
TAKE ME AS YOU FIND,
A GENTLEMAN OF HONOUR
I'M CARING AND I'M KIND.
I'LL HELP YOU IF I'M ABLE,
A SHOULDER FOR YOUR TEARS,
A SMILE TO MAKE YOU HAPPY
THERE THROUGH ALL THE YEARS.
ALL I HAVE TO GIVE,
IS ALWAYS THERE FOR YOU,
MY FRIENDSHIP AND MY LOYALTY
IS LONG LASTING AND TRUE.
I MAY NOT BE THE HANDSOME PRINCE,
TO TAKE YOU FAR AWAY,
BUT I'LL EVER BE THAT ONE TRUE FRIEND
AND HERE I'LL ALWAYS STAY.

14. SECRETS

WHERE DO YOU GO IN YOUR DREAMS
ALONE IN YOUR BED WHILE YOU SLEEP
WHO ARE YOU WITH AND WHAT DO YOU SEE
WHAT ARE THE SECRETS YOU KEEP?

WHAT DO YOU DO WITH YOUR DREAMS
THE MOMENT YOU WAKE FROM YOUR SLEEP
DO YOU FORGET OR DO YOU RECALL
OR ARE THEY JUST SECRETS TO KEEP?

WHAT ARE THE DREAMS YOU ARE DREAMING
EACH NIGHT WHILE YOU ARE ASLEEP
ARE THEY THE TRUTH AND DO THEY MAKE SENSE
AND ARE THEY JUST SECRETS WE KEEP?

15. THE REASON...?

WHAT'S THE POINT OF MEMORIES
WITH NO ONE YOU CAN SHARE
STARING OUT A WINDOW
OR AT AN EMPTY CHAIR
WHAT'S THE POINT OF MEMORIES
THEY JUST MIGHT CAUSE DISTRESS
THEY COULD BE ONE'S OF SADNESS
OR ONE'S OF HAPPINESS
WHAT'S THE POINT OF MEMORIES
MADE UP OF YOUR PAST
IF NO ONE UNDERSTANDS THEM
AS THEY DISAPPEAR QUITE FAST
WHAT'S THE USE OF MEMORIES
WHEN NO ONE'S THERE TO CARE
WHAT YOU DO TOMORROW
WITH WHO, WITH WHAT OR WHERE
WHAT'S THE USE OF MEMORIES
WHEN YOU JUST MIGHT RECALL
THINGS THAT HAPPENED LONG AGO
WHEN YOU WERE VERY SMALL
WHAT'S THE USE OF MEMORIES
WHAT CAN THEY DO FOR YOU
THE POINT OF ALL YOUR MEMORIES
IS...THEY'RE PART OF ALL YOU DO.

16. WHERE DO YOU GO?

TWO BY TWO THE SOCKS WENT IN
ALONG WITH OTHER CLOTHES
T-SHIRTS, TROUSERS, UNDERPANTS
A WASHING PILE SOON GROWS
ALL WENT IN THE WASH THAT DAY
AND ROUND AND ROUND IT SPUN
WASHING POWDER, WATER
THE CYCLE HAD BEGUN
TO GET ALL OF MY WASHING CLEAN
THE SUDS FLOWED FAST AND FREE
IT SEEMED TO TAKE FOREVER
AND SO I HAD SOME TEA
THE WASHING RINSED, THE WASHING SPUN
NO TIME TO MESS ABOUT
I TOOK ALL OF MY WASHING
AND WENT TO HANG IT OUT
PIECE BY PIECE I HUNG IT THERE
A BREEZE WAS BLOWING THROUGH
I PICKED THE SOCKS UP ONE BY ONE
INSTEAD OF TWO BY TWO
I COULDN'T FIND A MATCHING PAIR
ALTHOUGH I SEARCHED ABOUT
THE BASKET NOW WAS EMPTY
AND EVERYTHING WAS OUT
WITH ALL THE WASHING HANGING THERE
AND LOOKING VERY NEAT
I NOW WAS LEFT WITH SINGLE SOCKS
ALTHOUGH I HAVE TWO FEET!

17. A WEAPON OF WAR?

THE COMIC BOOK HERO
WHO ALWAYS FOUGHT CRIME
NOW LIVING A LIFE
IN A DIFFERENT TIME
GONE ARE THE DAYS
HE FOUGHT FOR THE GOOD
FIGHTING THE "BADDIES"
WITHOUT SPILLING BLOOD
THE EVIL HAS CHANGED
IT'S DIFFERENT NOW
CAN IT BE STOPPED
AND DO WE KNOW HOW?
NOT SUPERMAN POWERS
THAT COME FROM ABOVE
BUT THE GREATEST KNOWN WEAPON
IS SIMPLY CALLED LOVE.

18. THE ROAD.

SOMETIMES I WONDER WHERE I'VE BEEN
I'VE TRAVELLED FAR AND LONG
AND WONDER WHERE I'M GOING TO
WHERE DOES MY SOUL BELONG?
I'VE HAD SOME UPS AND HAD SOME DOWNS
I'VE SEEN A LOT OF THINGS
SOMETIMES MY HEAD IS WEARY
AT TIMES MY HEART JUST SINGS
LIFE IT HAS SURPRISES
AND SOME OF THEM ARE BAD
BUT SOME WILL MAKE ME LAUGH OUT LOUD
AND OTHERS MAKE ME SAD
I CANNOT CHANGE WHAT'S HAPPENED
FOR THAT IS NOW LONG GONE
AND WHO KNOWS WHAT THE FUTURE HOLDS
IT COULD BE RIGHT OR WRONG
BUT WHILE I HAVE THE PRESENT
TO SHAPE AND MOLD MY WAY
I'LL MAKE IT WHAT I WANT IT
IT'S NOT JUST FOR TODAY
FOR WHAT WE DO THIS DAYTIME
IS SHAPING WHAT'S TO COME
IT STARTS TO MAKE OUR FUTURE
AND CANNOT BE UNDONE.

19. BOUNCING ABOUT.

WHEN I WAS VERY LITTLE
THERE'S SOMETHING THAT I LEARNT
HUMANS DO NOT BOUNCE THAT WELL
THEY GET THEIR FINGERS BURNT
SO WHY NOW THAT I'M OLDER
I JUST SEEM TO FORGET
THAT BOUNCING IS NOT GOOD FOR ME
NOT EVEN FOR A BET!
COULD IT BE THE DRINK INSIDE
OR AM I GOING MAD?
OR AM I JUST PLAIN CRAZY
AND ACTING LIKE A LAD
FOR WHEN I TRY AND BOUNCE AROUND
I HEAR A FUNNY NOISE
IS THAT BONES I'M BREAKING
AND DOING IT BY CHOICE
OR IS IT JUST ARTHRITIS
MY JOINTS DON'T MOVE SO WELL
I SHOULD JUST STOP THE BOUNCING
OK, SO I JUST FELL!

20. LOST!

FROM A TO B AND B TO C
THE ROAD SHOULD BE SO STRAIGHT
BELIEVE ME FOLKS THAT JUST AIN'T SO
DIVERSIONS MAKE ME LATE.
DRIVING DOWN SOME COUNTRY ROADS
I DO NOT EVEN KNOW
FINDING JUNCTIONS LEFT AND RIGHT
WHICH WAY SHOULD I GO?
MOVING FORWARD SLOWLY
I FEEL I'M GOING BACK
AND THEN BEFORE I KNOW IT
I'M ON AN OLD DIRT TRACK.
I WONDER WILL I EVER REACH
THE PLACE I'M MEANT TO BE
OR WILL I DRIVE IN CIRCLES
OR END UP IN THE SEA?
WHY DO THEY MAKE DIVERSIONS
AND THINK THAT WE ALL KNOW
THE ROADS THAT THEY THEN SEND US DOWN
AND KNOW JUST WHERE TO GO.
PLEASE PUT UP MORE DIRECTIONS
AND HELP ME ON MY WAY
OR I MIGHT FIND THAT I AM LOST
FOREVER AND A DAY.

21. TO SLEEP.

WHEN TODAY IS OVER
AND SLEEP HAS HIT MY EYES
MY HEAD UPON THE PILLOW
MY HEART NO LONGER SIGHS
RESTFUL SLUMBER HITS ME
I DRIFT SO FAR AWAY
DREAMS WILL TAKE ME WITH THEM
AT THE CLOSING OF THE DAY
TO LEAVE BEHIND MY WORRIES
AND TAKE AWAY MY FEARS
RESTING, SLEEPING PEACEFULLY
AND TAKE AWAY MY TEARS.
GOOD NIGHT, GOD BLESS MY DEAR FRIENDS
I HOPE YOU TOO FIND REST
AND IN THE MORNING SUNSHINE
BE FEELING AT OUR BEST.

22. FOUR MONTHS.

WAS IT SOMETHING THAT I DID
OR SOMETHING THAT I SAID?
DID I GO WRONG SOMEWHERE
OR WAS I JUST MISLED?
I STILL DON'T HAVE THE ANSWER
I DO NOT KNOW THE WAY
I GO ON WALKING BLINDLY
SLOWLY DAY BY DAY.
NO ONE TAKES ME BY THE HAND
AND NO ONE DRIES MY TEARS
WITH NO ONE THERE TO COMFORT ME
AND TAKE AWAY MY FEARS
I MAKE MY WAY ALONG ALONE
AND TRY TO UNDERSTAND
WHERE IT IS I'M GOING
AND WHERE IT IS I STAND
I TRY TO TALK ABOUT IT
I TRY TO STATE MY CASE
BUT NO ONE SEEMS TO LISTEN
OR LOOK ME IN THE FACE
I KNOW THAT I AM NOT ALONE
THERE'S OTHERS JUST LIKE ME
BUT NO ONE SEEMS TO NOTICE
OR JUST DON'T WANT TO SEE
IT ONLY TAKES A SIMPLE WORD
OR JUST A LITTLE SMILE
TO HELP US ON THE LONELY ROAD
WE TRAVEL MILE BY MILE.

23. TWO LOVERS.

UNDERNEATH THE STARS AT NIGHT
THE WORLD IS HIDDEN OUT OF SIGHT
A GENTLE BREEZE BLOWS THROUGH THE LONG DRY GRASS
THE MOON SHINES IN THE SKY ABOVE
TWO LOVERS SIT THERE SO IN LOVE
A GENTLE FELLOW AND HIS GENTLE LASS

HOLDING HANDS OH SO TIGHT
THE HOURS SOON ARE TAKING FLIGHT
THE NIGHT TIME QUICKLY FADES INTO THE DAWN
THE AIR IS COOL THEY CUDDLE CLOSE
NO ONE SEES AND NO ONE KNOWS
AS THEY SIT THERE IN THE EARLY MORN.

UNDERNEATH THE EARLY SUN
AS THE NEW DAY HAS BEGUN
THE BIRDS START SINGING HIGH UP IN THE SKY
TWO LOVERS START TO FADE AWAY
SHADOWS AT THE BREAK OF DAY
LOVERS FROM AN AGE THAT'S LONG GONE BY.

24. WHERE TO...?

WHERE DO WE GO FROM HERE
AS WE'RE TRAVELLING YEAR TO YEAR
WE'VE GOT TO STAY SAFE
AND WE'VE GOT TO STAY STRONG
THE ROAD THAT WE TRAVEL
IS WINDING AND LONG
SO WHERE DO WE GO FROM HERE.

WHERE DO WE GO FROM HERE
WE'VE NOTHING TO LOSE OR TO FEAR
WE CANNOT STAND STILL
WE'VE GOT TO MOVE ON
THE JOURNEY WE'RE TAKING
IS SO VERY LONG
AND WHERE DO WE GO FROM HERE

WHERE DO WE GO FROM HERE
TRAVELLING FAR AND NEAR
SOMETIMES ALL ALONE
SOMETIMES WITH A FRIEND
THE ROAD THAT WE TRAVEL
JUST HAS NO END
SO WHERE DO WE GO FROM HERE.

25. IF...

IF YOU CRY IN THE DARK
WILL ANYONE HEAR?
IF YOU REACH OUT YOUR HAND
IS ANYONE NEAR?
IF YOU LOOK FOR A STAR
WILL CLOUDS FILL THE SKY?
IF YOU REACH FOR THE MOON
WILL THE DAY PASS YOU BY?
IF YOUR TEARS FALL LIKE RAIN
WILL YOU WIPE THEM AWAY?
IF A SMILE FILLS YOUR FACE
DO YOU THINK IT WILL STAY?
IF YOU'RE FEELING LOST
WHERE DO YOU GO?
IF YOU NEED AND ANSWER
DOES ANYONE KNOW?
IF ALL DREAMS COME TRUE
WILL EVERYONE SLEEP?
IF YOU CRY IN THE DARK
ARE THEY DREAMS YOU CAN KEEP?

26. THE FRIGHT OF MY LIFE!

IF MY TEDDY CAME TO LIFE
AND HUGGED ME VERY TIGHT
I'D SCREAM AND SHOUT OR RUN AWAY
AND STAY AWAKE ALL NIGHT!
I'D SHAKE AND I WOULD TREMBLE
AND WOULDN'T WANT TO SLEEP
I'D JUST KEEP LOOKING ALL ABOUT
IN CASE I CAUGHT A PEEP
TEDDIES SHOULDN'T COME TO LIFE
IT REALLY SCARES ME SO
I WILL NOT GO TO BED TONIGHT
ALTHOUGH I OUGHT TO GO.
I WILL NOT SLEEP SO EASILY
I WILL NOT EVEN REST
JUST IN CASE MY TEDDY BEAR
PUTS ME TO THE TEST!
IF MY TEDDY CAME TO LIFE
I'D THROW HIM OUT THE DOOR
I COULDN'T LOVE MY TEDDY BEAR
OR WANT HIM ANYMORE.

POOR TEDDY!

27. JOIN ME!

IF YOU GO DOWN TO THE WOODS TODAY
YOU JUST MIGHT GET A SURPRISE
FOR I MIGHT BE THERE TOTALLY NUDE
DANCING BEFORE YOUR EYES
FOR I'M FEELING CRAZY AND WANT TO GO MAD
I SIMPLY JUST DON'T GIVE A DAMN
I'M FED UP WITH BEING STRAIGHT LACED AND GOOD
I JUST WANT TO BE A FREE MAN
I WANT TO BE HAPPY, I WANT TO BE BRIGHT
AND DO THINGS TO JUST PLEASE MYSELF
FOR TOO MANY YEARS I'VE DONE AS I'M TOLD
NOW IT'S TIME TO COME DOWN OFF THE SHELF
IF YOU GO DOWN TO THE WOODS TODAY
YOU'VE BEEN WARNED OF THINGS YOU MIGHT SEE
AND IF YOU TOO WANT TO GO MAD
THEN WHY DON'T YOU COME AND JOIN ME!

28. THE COURAGE YOU DON'T LACK

FACE THE WORLD AND FACE YOUR FEARS
THERE MIGHT BE WORSE TO COME
TAKE YOUR HEART, TAKE YOUR MIND
JUST DO WHAT MUST BE DONE
TAKE A STEP AND THEN ONE MORE
AS HARD AS IT MAY BE
NO ONE'S REALLY WATCHING YOU
WELL WHO CARES WHAT THEY SEE
HAVE THEY FACED THE SAME FEARS?
AND BEEN THERE ALL ALONE
WALKING IN THE DARKNESS
AND FACING THE UNKNOWN
IT MAY TAKE LOTS OF COURAGE
IT'S SOMETHING YOU DON'T LACK
JUST FACE TOWARD THE FUTURE
MAKE SURE YOU DON'T LOOK BACK
AND AS YOU MAKE THAT FIRST STEP
THE NEXT ONE'S NOT SO BAD
ALTHOUGH YOU MOVE ON SLOWLY
YOU'LL FIND IT MAKES YOU GLAD
GLAD YOU MADE THE EFFORT -

GLAD YOU TOOK A CHANCE -

GLAD THAT YOU'RE BACK LIVING -

AND JOINING IN LIFE'S DANCE.

29. ME!

I HAVE TO BE BRAVE
I HAVE TO BE STRONG
WHO IS TO JUDGE
IF I'M RIGHT OR I'M WRONG?
I HAVE TO DECIDE
I HAVE TO CHOOSE
IF I MAKE MISTAKES
IT'S I WHO WILL LOSE
I HAVE THE WILL
I HAVE THE RIGHT
IT'S TIME TO STAND UP
I HAVE TO FIGHT
I CAN BE ANYTHING
I WANT TO BE
I CAN DO ANYTHING
JUST WATCH AND SEE
AM I THE PERSON
YOU WANT TO SEE?
WELL I HAVE A LIFE
AND THAT PERSON IS ME!

30. THE WHOLE WORLD AND ME.

IF THE WHOLE WORLD STARTED LOVING
THE CHANGES THERE WOULD BE
NO MORE GRIEF AND SORROW
OR FEAR OF WHAT MIGHT BE
WE'D HAVE THE CHANCE TO LIVE IN PEACE
WITH NO MORE TEARS AND PAIN
AND TIME FOR ONE ANOTHER
WITHOUT THE GREED OR GAIN
WITH TIME TO STOP AND SAY "HELLO!"
OR GIVE A CHEERY SMILE
TIME FOR ONE ANOTHER
FOR JUST A LITTLE WHILE
THE GREATEST GIFTS THAT'S GIVEN
TO EVERYONE AROUND
THE GIFTS OF LOVE AND CARING
THE GREATEST GIFTS I'VE FOUND.

31. FREE TO BE

I SEE THE TEARS BEHIND YOUR EYES
YOU DO NOT LET THEM GO
THE SMILE YOU HAVE UPON YOUR FACE
IS FALSE, OF THAT I KNOW
YOU HOLD BACK YOUR EMOTIONS
YOU KEEP THEM HID AWAY
AND ONLY LET YOUR FEELINGS OUT
AT CLOSING OF THE DAY
YOU DO NOT SHARE THEM WITH US
AFRAID THAT WE MIGHT SEE
JUST WHAT IS GOING THROUGH YOUR MIND
BE BRAVE AND LET THEM BE
DO NOT EVER WORRY
WHAT OTHERS THINK OF YOU
BE YOURSELF THE BEST YOU CAN
AND DO WHAT YOU MUST DO
YOU ARE YOU AND STAY THAT WAY
JUST AS I AM ME
NO MATTER WHAT YOU HAVE TO DO
LIVE YOUR LIFE BE FREE.

32. FIRST THE GOOD NEWS...

THERE ISN'T ANY GOOD NEWS BUT...

THERE'S BAD NEWS ON THE FRONT PAGE
AND BAD NEWS ON THE SCREEN
IS THERE ANY GOOD NEWS
THAT ANYBODY'S SEEN
WE SEEM TO THRIVE ON BAD NEWS
WE SEE IT EVERY DAY
HOW OFTEN IS THERE GOOD NEWS
HEADED RIGHT OUR WAY
BAD NEWS HEARD FROM OVERSEAS
BAD NEWS HERE AT HOME
BAD NEWS ALL AROUND US NOW
WHEREVER WE MAY ROAM
I WANT TO HEAR SOME GOOD NEWS
JUST TO MAKE ME SMILE
LET'S FORGET THE BAD NEWS
FOR A LITTLE WHILE.

33. FORGOTTEN DREAMS.

CHILDHOOD DREAMS AND FANTASIES
WE LEAVE THEM FAR BEHIND
LEAVING DISTANT MEMORIES
OF THINGS WE CANNOT FIND
SIMPLICITY AND INNOCENCE
WE LOSE ALONG THE WAY
SLIPPING THROUGH OUR FINGERS
WHILE GROWING DAY BY DAY
CHILDHOOD DREAMS AND INNOCENCE
COULD TEACH US QUITE A LOT
TEACH US THINGS WE USED TO KNOW
THINGS WE'VE NOW FORGOT.

34. THROUGH THE YEARS.

I JUST LOOKED BACK AT MEMORIES
OUR DREAMS OF YESTERDAY
THE THINGS WE DID TOGETHER
GOING ON OUR WAY
THE HAPPY SMILES TOGETHER
WALKING HAND IN HAND
DOWN ALONG A COUNTRY LANE
OR WALKING ON THE SAND.
MAKING PLANS TOGETHER
FOR THINGS THAT WE WOULD DO
THINGS WE'D OFTEN DONE BEFORE
AND THINGS THAT WERE QUITE NEW
HOW QUICKLY NOW THAT TIME HAS PASSED
WHERE HAVE THE YEARS ALL GONE
DAYS AND MONTHS ARE GOING BY
QUICKLY ONE BY ONE
AND ALL THAT I HAVE NOW GOT LEFT
TO TAKE ME THROUGH THE YEARS
ARE FOND REMEMBERED MEMORIES
THE LAUGHTER AND THE TEARS

35. THIS MAN!

THIS IS THE MAN THAT I AM
FINALLY SET FREE
I'LL DO THE THINGS THAT I WANT
BE WHAT I WANT TO BE
HE HID AWAY BENEATH ME
AND KEPT WELL OUT OF SIGHT
BUT NOW THE MAN IS BREAKING FREE
NOW THE TIME IS RIGHT

SOME PEOPLE MAY BE SHOCKED
AND NOT LIKE WHAT THEY SEE
OR NOT LIKE WHAT THEY HEAR
BUT THIS MAN NOW IS ME.

THIS IS THE MAN THAT I AM
AND GROWING VERY FAST
HEADED FOR MY FUTURE
TO LEAVE BEHIND MY PAST
MAKING MANY CHANGES
AND CHOICES ON THE WAY
MOVING SLOWLY FORWARD
LIVING DAY TO DAY.

SOME PEOPLE MAY BE SHOCKED
AND NOT WANT ME TO BE
WHAT I AM BECOMING
BUT THIS MAN NOW IS ME

THIS IS THE MAN THAT I AM
I'M PROUD OF ALL I'VE DONE
I FOUGHT AGAINST THE ODDS NOW
AND FINALLY I'VE WON
I'VE MADE A LOT OF CHANGES
BECOME A BRAND NEW MAN
AND THO' THE TIMES WERE HARD
I'VE DONE THE BEST I CAN

SOME PEOPLE MAY BE SHOCKED
BUT THIS MAN HERE IS FREE
AND DOING WHAT HE WANTS TO
AND THIS MAN NOW IS ME.

36. FALLEN HERO.

THE WIND WAS BLOWING THROUGH THE TREES
THE SNOW BEGAN TO FALL
THE PARK WAS DARK AND LONELY
WITH NO ONE THERE AT ALL
NO ONE BUT THE OLD MAN
WHO WANDERED THERE ALONE
LOOKING FOR A PLACE TO REST
A BENCH TO CALL HIS HOME
PAPERS FOR HIS BLANKETS
NO PILLOW FOR HIS HEAD
A COLD HARD BENCH WAS ALL HE HAD
THAT HE COULD CALL A BED.
TIRED NOW AND WEARY
NO FOOD FOR HIM TO EAT
LIVING OUT HIS OLD DAYS
ON THE LONELY STREET
HOW COULD A HERO FALL SO FAR?
FORGOTTEN IN THIS DAY
SOMEONE ONCE WHO GAVE HIS ALL
FORGOTTEN IN THIS WAY.

37. WATCHING

EVERY NIGHT AND EVERY DAY
SOMEONE CALLS TO ME TO SAY
"WHERE YOU GOING, WHERE YOU BEEN
AND ARE YOU COMING BACK AGAIN."
EVERY DAY AND EVERY NIGHT
SOMEONE WHO'S JUST OUT OF SIGHT
KNOWS WHERE I AM, WHERE I'VE BEEN
AND KNOWS THE THINGS I'VE DONE AND SEEN
WHO IT IS I CANNOT SAY
BUT THERE THEY ARE EVERY DAY
WATCHING ME AND WATCHING YOU
WATCHING EVERYTHING WE DO.

38. SWEET SHOP MEMORIES

SHERBET FOUNTAINS, SHERBET DABS
FIREMANS LACES TOO
A HAZELNUT IN EVERY BITE
AND CHERRIES IN IT TOO
THAT WAS TOPIC CHOCOLATE BAR
MARS BAR, MILKY WAY
THE MILKY BAR KID ON OUR SCREENS
ALMOST EVERY DAY
SPANGLES SWEETS IN LIQUORICE
FRUITY FLAVOURS TOO
MELT IN YOUR MOUTH NOT IN YOUR HAND
THAT'S WHAT A TREET WOULD DO
A JAMBOREE BAG NOW AND THEN
WOULD BE A SPECIAL TREAT
RAINBOW DROPS FROM OUT THE CONE
WE ATE UPON THE STREET
DO YOU REMEMBER GOBSTOPPERS
HOW THE COLOUR CHANGED
AND BALLS MADE OUT OF ANISEED
FROM JARS SO WELL ARRANGED.
I REMEMBER WALNUT WHIPS
HAD WALNUTS IN AND OUT
BAZOOKA WAS THE BUBBLE GUM
OF THAT WE HAD NO DOUBT
PALMA VIOLETS, LOVE HEARTS
COST A PENNY TOO
ALL THESE SWEETS AND MANY MORE
JUST FOR ME AND YOU!

39. SIMPLY PUT.

ALL I WANT IS SIMPLE THINGS
A SIMPLE LIFE
WITHOUT THE STRINGS
A GENTLE LIFE WITH GENTLE WAYS
HASSLE FREE
TO LIVE MY DAYS
GOLDEN SUNSETS EVERY NIGHT
TO TAKE THE DAY
WELL OUT OF SIGHT
GENTLE MOONBEAMS IN THE SKY
A GENTLE BREEZE
JUST DRIFTING BY
SIMPLE THINGS LIKE BUTTERFLIES
FLITTING BY
IN SUMMER SKIES
PRETTY FLOWERS WILD AND FREE
GROWING THERE
FOR ALL TO SEE
I WANT TO LIVE A SIMPLE LIFE
WITHOUT THE STRESS
WITHOUT THE STRIFE
WATCHING CLOUDS DRIFTING BY
CHANGING SHAPES
UP IN THE SKY
SMILING BRIGHTLY EVERY DAY
LIVING LIFE
IN MY OWN WAY
A SIMPLE LIFE WITH SIMPLE WAYS
SIMPLY LIVED
THROUGH ALL MY DAYS.

40. VOICE OF THE HEART

THE DAY WAS VERY QUIET
DOWN THE COUNTRY LANE
THERE WAS NO TIME FOR SORROW
THERE WAS NO TIME FOR PAIN
THE MEMORIES CAME FLOODING BACK
OF ALL THOSE YEARS AGO
CHILDREN I WOULD PLAY WITH
WE WATCHED EACH OTHER GROW
AND NOW I AM MUCH OLDER
TIME HAS NOW MOVED ON
PEOPLE THAT I ONCE KNEW
ALL OF THEM NOW GONE
BUT WHAT'S THAT NOISE I'M HEARING
VOICES DRAWING NEAR
THE SOUND OF CHILDREN'S LAUGHTER
COMING TO MY EAR
JUST DRIFTING SOUNDS FROM LONG AGO
IT'S JUST A MEMORY
THEY'RE VOICES PLAYING IN MY HEAD
WITH NOTHING THERE TO SEE
VOICES IN MY MEMORY
GIVING ME A START
SOUNDING LOUD AND CLEAR NOW
JUST VOICES OF THE HEART

41. LONELY FOOLS

TOO MANY HEARTACHES
AND TOO MANY FOOLS
TRYING TOO HARD
THEY'RE BREAKING THE RULES
LONELY AND DISTANT
AND LIVING APART
HOLDING ON TIGHT
TO ONE BREAKING HEART
THEY WANT TO LET GO
BUT DO NOT KNOW HOW
SOMETIME IN THE FUTURE
BUT SHOULD DO IT NOW
THE ROAD THAT THEY'RE WALKING
IS LONELY AND LONG
THEY HAVE TO BE WISE
THEY NEED TO BE STRONG
IT COMES TO THE END
WITH ONE BROKEN HEART
BEING TOGETHER
YET BEING APART.

42. SECOND BEST

PEOPLE SAY I SHOULD BE HAPPY
WITH MY MEMORIES
THEY SAY I SHOULD BE GRATEFUL
FOR ALL MY "USED TO BE'S"
BUT YOU CANNOT HOLD A MEMORY
AND HUG IT CLOSE AND TIGHT
YOU CANNOT KISS A MEMORY
TO WISH IT A GOODNIGHT
YOU CANNOT LISTEN TO ITS HEART
WHILE RESTING ON ITS CHEST
ALL THE MEMORIES THAT YOU HAVE
ARE ONLY SECOND BEST
SECOND TO THE ONE YOU LOVED
FOR ALL THOSE MANY YEARS
AND UNLIKE ALL THOSE MEMORIES
NEVER BROUGHT YOU TEARS.

43. WISHES AND DREAMS

IF DREAMS CAME FROM WISHES
AND WISHES CAME TRUE
ALL THAT YOU DREAMED OF
WOULD SOON COME TO YOU
WISHES ON STARS
OR DREAMS IN THE NIGHT
ALL THAT YOU HOPE FOR
IS WELL WITHIN SIGHT
REACH FOR YOUR WISHES
AND NEVER GIVE IN
FOLLOW YOUR DREAMS
YOU KNOW YOU CAN WIN.

44. I SAW...I HEARD...

I SAW YOUR SMILE
I HEARD YOUR LAUGH
BUT I LOOKED AT
A PHOTOGRAPH.

I SAW YOUR FACE
I HEARD YOUR VOICE
AN ECHO OF
THE SWEETEST NOISE.

I SAW YOUR EYES
I HEARD YOU SAY
WE'D MEET AGAIN
ANOTHER DAY.

I SAW YOU LEAVE
I HEARD YOU PART
BUT HERE YOU'LL STAY
DEEP IN MY HEART.

45. A FLICKER OF LIGHT.

FLICKERING CANDLES MAKING SHAPES
UPON A DARKENED WALL
A DANCING FLAME UPON A WICK
THAT REALLY IS QUITE SMALL
AND YET THE SHADOWS THAT THEY CAST
DANCING ON THE WALL
SEEM TO BE SO VERY LARGE
BEFORE THEY TAKE THE FALL
HOUR BY HOUR THE CANDLES SHRINK
THE LIGHT REMAINS A FLAME
CASTING SHADOWS LARGE AND SMALL
HOUR BY HOUR THE SAME
THE GLOW REMAINS THE CANDLES DIE
AND SLOWLY MELT AWAY
A FLICKERING LIGHT UPON A WICK
TO CLOSE ANOTHER DAY.

46. YOURS AND MINE

I MAY NOT BE STRONG
I MAY NOT BE WISE
BUT I SEE THE WORLD
THROUGH MY PAIR OF EYES
A WORLD GOING CRAZY
A WORLD GOING WRONG
A WORLD THAT HAS HATRED
WHERE LOVE SHOULD BELONG
AND I'M SEEING PEOPLE
RUSHING AROUND
WITH NO TIME TO STOP
THEY'RE JUST ONWARD BOUND
THEY'RE MISSING THE BEAUTY
AND MISSING OUT PEACE
NO TIME TO RELAX
THEY LIVE ILL AT EASE
THEY WORRY WHAT'S COMING
OR HOW THEY'LL SURVIVE
THEY'RE NOT EVEN GRATEFUL
THAT THEY ARE ALIVE
THEY TAKE IT FOR GRANTED
TOMORROW IS THEIRS
AND STILL GO ON RUSHING
WITH WORRIES AND CARES
I TOOK A STEP BACK
AND LIKED WHAT I SAW
A WORLD THAT HAS BEAUTY
AND VERY MUCH MORE
I OPEN MY ARMS
TO OFFER YOU LOVE
NOW OPEN YOUR EYES
TO THE PUSH AND THE SHOVE
STOP WHAT YOU'RE DOING
TAKE TIME TO PAUSE
THE LOVE AND THE PEACE
CAN BE MINE AND BE YOURS

47. SOMEONE TO BE

DON'T TALK TO ME - I DON'T WANT TO HEAR
DON'T LOOK AT ME OR I'LL CRY
AND DAY AFTER DAY - WEEK AFTER WEEK
YOU JUST SIMPLY PASS ME BY
DON'T LISTEN TO ME AND THE WORDS THAT I SAY
FOR SOME OF THEM JUST COME OUT WRONG
FOR HERE I AM AND HERE I'LL STAY
THIS IS WHERE I BELONG
I'M BEING BRIGHT AND I'M BEING BRAVE
WHILE I'M BEING ALL ALONE
MY HEART CRYING OUT SEARCHING FOR HELP
IS CERTAINLY NOT MADE OF STONE
LISTEN TO ME –DON'T LISTEN TO ME
MIXED UP AND SO CONFUSED
FEELING THE WORLD IS PASSING ME BY
LEAVING ME TIRED AND BRUISED
THE LIGHT THAT IS SHINING AND SO OUT OF REACH
SEEMS TO BE SO FAR AWAY
BUT SOMEONE IS THERE WAVING TO ME
I'M SEEING HIM EVERY DAY
HE CALLS OUT MY NAME AND REACHES FOR ME
GUIDING ME SLOWLY ALONG
AND EACH STEP I'M TAKING MOVING HIS WAY
I'M GROWING AND GOING TO BE STRONG.
A FRIEND WHO IS LOYAL A FRIEND WHO IS TRUE
SOMEONE TO STAND BESIDE ME
SOMEONE TO HELP IN MY HOUR OF NEED
AND SOMEONE WHO SIMPLY WILL BE.

48. SUNDAY EVENING.

SITTING IN AN OLD ARMCHAIR
A GLOW FROM THE FIRE LIGHT
BOOK IN HAND AND SLIPPERS ON
AWAY FROM THE COLD DARK NIGHT.
TURNING PAGES ONE BY ONE
SIPPING A CUP OF TEA
SUNDAY EVENING ALL ALONE
JUST THE DOG AND ME.
WITH NO ONE ON THE TELEPHONE
THE TV ISN'T ON
A LAZY WAY TO SPEND MY TIME
NOW THE DAY IS GONE.
WITH NO ONE HERE TO BOTHER ME
AND NOTHING ELSE TO DO
I'LL LAZE AWAY THE EVENING
YOU SHOULD DO IT TOO.

49. TOGETHER.

WE'RE STANDING HERE UPON THE EDGE
LOOKING OUT AT LIFE
SOME WITHOUT A HUSBAND
AND SOME WITHOUT A WIFE
OUR GRIEF IS SAILING CLOSE TO SHORE
BUT DRIFTING FURTHER ON
SOME DAYS WE DO NOT SEE IT
YET KNOW IT HASN'T GONE.
WE WALK ALONG THE EDGE OF LIFE
FEELING ALL ALONE
LOOKING FOR THE LOST SOUL
OF SOMEONE WE HAD KNOWN
WE DO NOT SEE THE OTHERS
WHO WALK THE PATH AS WELL
WE'RE BLINDED BY THE TEARS WE SHED
OUR LIFE AN EMPTY SHELL
THEN SOMEONE HOLDS A HAND OUT
SOMEONE WE DON'T KNOW
WE GRASP THE HAND IN FAITH AND HOPE
OUR STRENGTH BEGINS TO GROW
AND WITH OUR STRENGTH OUR COURAGE GROWS
WE START TO MAKE NEW FRIENDS
WE START TO FEEL NEW HAPPINESS
THOUGH SORROW NEVER ENDS
AND NOW WE STAND TOGETHER
LOOKING OUT AT LIFE
ONE WAS ONCE A HUSBAND
AND ONE WAS ONCE A WIFE
BUT NOW WE HAVE NEW FRIENDSHIP
WITH PEOPLE WHO CAN SHARE
PEOPLE BROUGHT TOGETHER
WHO SHOW THEY REALLY CARE
ALL GOING THROUGH THE SAME THINGS
WHILE LIVING DAY TO DAY
SUPPORTING ONE ANOTHER
WHILST GOING ON OUR WAY.

50. ANGELS.

WHEN THE RAIN FALLS FROM THE SKY
IS THAT WHEN THE ANGELS CRY
DO THEY CRY FOR WHAT WE DO
DO THEY CRY FOR ME AND YOU
WHEN THEY SMILE DO WE SEE
THEIR LIGHT SHINE DOWN ON YOU AND ME
ARE THEY HAPPY ARE THEY BRIGHT
DO THEY LAUGH WITH PURE DELIGHT
WATCHING US BOTH NIGHT AND DAY
HEARING EVERYTHING WE SAY
WATCHING OVER ME AND YOU
GUARDING US IN ALL WE DO
THANK THE ANGELS EVERY DAY
FOR GUARDING US IN THEIR OWN WAY
THANK THE ANGELS EVERY NIGHT
FOR KEEPING US WITHIN THEIR SIGHT

51. POETRY IN MOTION

WHO KNOWS WHAT'S INSIDE MY HEAD
GOING ROUND AND ROUND
IT JUST POPS OUT ONTO THE PAGE
WITHOUT A SINGLE SOUND
WRITTEN WORDS JUST FLOWING OUT
IN RHYTHM AND IN RHYME
FLOWING FREELY LINE BY LINE
EVERY SINGLE TIME.
WHERE THEY COME FROM I DON'T KNOW
I HAVE TO SET THEM FREE
I CANNOT STOP THEM BEING WROTE
THEY JUST COME OUT OF ME
I HAVEN'T TIME TO STOP AND THINK
WHEN THEY'RE COMING ON
FOR IF I DO I JUST FIND OUT
THE WHOLE THING SIMPLY GONE

52. SHOW THE WORLD.

YOU CANNOT RUN
YOU CANNOT HIDE
FROM THE DEMONS
HID INSIDE
YOU MAY NOT LIKE
THE THINGS YOU SEE
THEY'RE STILL A PART
OF YOU OR ME
YOU MAY NOT LIKE
THE THINGS YOU HEAR
ECHO SOUNDS
WITHIN YOUR EAR
YOU SAY THE THINGS
YOU HAVE TO SAY
TO GET YOU THROUGH
FROM DAY TO DAY
YOU FIND THE COURAGE
LOSE THE FEAR
TAKE WHAT'S YOURS
AND HOLD IT NEAR
SO DO NOT RUN
STAND PROUD AND TALL
AND SHOW THE WORLD
YOU HAVE IT ALL.

53. HELP WANTED!

CAN SOMEONE HELP MY RESTLESS SOUL
IT REALLY NEEDS TO FLY
TO BREAK THE CHAINS AND SPREAD ITS WINGS
SOAR AWAY ON HIGH.
CAN SOMEONE FIND THE MISSING PARTS
FROM MY BROKEN HEART
PUT IT BACK TOGETHER
TO MAKE A BRAND NEW START.
CAN SOMEONE OPEN UP MY EYES
HELP THE BLIND TO SEE
THE WORLD CAN BE A BETTER PLACE
ESPECIALLY FOR ME.
CAN SOMEONE TAKE ME BY THE HAND
AND LEAD ME GENTLY ON
SHOW ME WHERE I'M GOING
MY ROAD IS DARK AND LONG
CAN SOMEONE LIGHT A CANDLE
TO CHASE AWAY THE DARK
PUT A SMILE BACK ON MY FACE
IT ONLY TAKES A SPARK.
CAN SOMEONE BE A FRIEND TO ME
AND NEVER TURN AWAY
BE TRUE, BE KIND BE LOYAL
BE IT NIGHT OR DAY.

54. A NEW WORLD

THE GRASS IS TURNING GREENER
THERE'S FLOWERS OUT IN BLOOM
THE SUN IS SHINING IN THE SKY
TO LIFT THE WINTER GLOOM
SPRING IS NOW UPON US
LIFTING SPIRITS HIGH
THE WORLD IS WAKING FROM ITS SLEEP
WE HEAVE A THANKFUL SIGH
ANOTHER WINTER OVER
AND SPRING IS IN THE AIR
BIRDS START SINGING IN THE TREES
THEIR SONG IS OURS TO SHARE
A NEW WORLD NOW IS STARTING
LIKE WAKING FROM A SLEEP
TAKING US ALL FORWARD
RISING FROM THE DEEP.

55. SHOULD I?

SHOULD I STOP BELIEVING
WHEN EVERYTHING GOES WRONG?
OR SHOULD I MOVE ON FORWARD
TO WHERE I SHOULD BELONG?
SHOULD I STOP BELIEVING
WHEN SKIES ARE TURNING GREY?
OR SHOULD I FIND THE SUNSHINE
TO BRIGHTEN UP MY DAY?
SHOULD I STOP BELIEVING
WHEN I'M FEELING LOST?
OR SHOULD I KEEP ON TRYING
NO MATTER WHAT THE COST?
SHOULD I STOP BELIEVING
WHEN ALL SEEMS SO UNFAIR?
OR SHOULD I JUST LIFT UP MY HEAD
AS IF I DO NOT CARE?
SHOULD I STOP BELIEVING
OR SHOULD I JUST GO ON?
I WILL NOT STOP BELIEVING
I'M HERE WHERE I BELONG.

56. FOOLS ERRAND

I'VE BEEN A FOOL
FOR MOST OF MY LIFE
CHASING THE RAINBOWS
THROUGH TROUBLE AND STRIFE
LOOKING FOR ANSWERS
SEARCHING FOR TRUTH
FROM CHILDHOOD TO ADULT
WHEN I WAS A YOUTH
STILL I KEEP SEARCHING
HOPING TO FIND
IS IT FOR REAL
OR JUST IN MY MIND
FOR WHAT I AM LOOKING
I DON'T EVEN KNOW
AND JUST KEEP ON SEARCHING
WHEREVER I GO

57. FRAGILE.

IF LIFE WAS MARKED AS FRAGILE
WOULD WE TAKE MORE CARE?
HANDLE IT WITH GENTLENESS
AS WE TAKE AND SHARE,
WOULD WE LOOK AT WHAT WE DO
AND CHANGE WHAT THINGS ARE BAD?
TRY AND BE MUCH BETTER
AND LOOK AT WHAT WE HAD,
WOULD WE LOOK AT WHAT WE'VE LOST?
THINGS WE DON'T HAVE NOW,
AND CARE FOR WHAT WE NOW HAVE LEFT
NO MATTER WHERE OR HOW?
OR IS IT THAT WE JUST DON'T CARE
AND THAT WE JUST CAN'T SEE?
THAT LIFE IS VERY FRAGILE
FOR YOU, FOR THEM, FOR ME.

58. TRUE FRIENDSHIP

THERE IS NO RIVER WE CAN'T CROSS
NO MOUNTAIN WE CAN'T CLIMB
WE'VE HAD TO DO IT ALL BEFORE
WE'LL DO IT EVERY TIME
THERE IS NO GOAL WE CANNOT REACH
NO AIM FOR US TOO HIGH
WE'LL JUST KEEP GO ON REACHING
UNTIL WE TOUCH THE SKY
THERE IS NO ROAD TOO LONG FOR US
THERE'S NOTHING BLOCKS OUR WAY
WE'LL BATTLE THROUGH THE DARKEST NIGHTS
UNTIL THE LIGHT OF DAY
THERE IS NO WINTER COLD ENOUGH
NOR SUMMER BE TOO HOT
WE'LL ALL JUST KEEP ON GOING
WITH EVERYTHING WE'VE GOT
THERE'S NOTHING COMES BETWEEN US
AND CAN'T KEEP US APART
TRUE FRIENDSHIP BUILT THROUGHOUT THE YEARS
STRONG RIGHT FROM THE START.

59. SPRINGTIME

BLUE SKIES AND SUNSHINE
CAN FOOL THE WAKING MIND
EVEN THOUGH THE WINTER COLD
ISN'T FAR BEHIND
FLUFFY CLOUDS AND BRIGHTEST SUN
TO OPEN UP OUR EYES
CAN EVEN FOOL THE SMALLEST BIRDS
FLYING IN THE SKIES
DRIFTING SLOWLY PASSING ON
TIME KEEPS MARCHING BY
NOTHING STOPS THE SEASONS
THE YEARS TOO QUICKLY FLY
DARK CLOUDS FOLLOW GREY CLOUDS
AND WINDS BEGIN TO BLOW
THE COLD ONCE MORE UPON US
AND NOTHING SEEMS TO GROW
WE WAIT WITH GROWING PATIENCE
FOR SKIES OF BLUE AND SUN
AND LISTEN FOR THE FIRST BIRDS
TO KNOW SPRING HAS BEGUN.

60. ESCAPE.

SOMETIMES I WANT TO JUST ESCAPE
AND HIDE AWAY FROM LIFE
COVER UP THE DAY TIMES
MY TROUBLES AND MY STRIFE
SOMETIMES I WANT TO RUN AWAY
AND HIDE FROM EVERYTHING
WIPE AWAY THE TEARS THAT FALL
THAT HAVE A BITTER STING.

SOMETIMES I WANT TO JUST ESCAPE
FROM WHAT I HAVE TO FACE
AND FIND I'M MANY YEARS AWAY
AND IN A BETTER PLACE
SOMETIMES I WANT TO JUST LIE DOWN
AND SLEEP THE DAY AWAY
AND HOPE THAT IN THE MORNING LIGHT
WILL BE A BRIGHTER DAY

SOMETIMES I WANT TO JUST ESCAPE
AND BE HERE WITH MY PEACE
WITH NO ONE NEAR TO BOTHER ME
AND MAKE MY SILENCE CEASE
SOMETIMES I DON'T KNOW WHAT I WANT
AND DON'T KNOW WHAT TO DO
SOMETIMES I WANT TO JUST ESCAPE
AND START MY LIFE ANEW.

61. FOR YOU, IT'S YOURS.

YOU BE BRAVE
YOU BE STRONG
EVEN WHEN YOU'RE TOLD
YOU'RE WRONG
YOU CAN RUN
YOU CAN FLY
YOU NEED TO REACH OUT
TOUCH THE SKY
HEAR YOUR HEART
HEAR YOUR MIND
SEARCH FOR TRUTH
AND YOU WILL FIND
YOU CAN HAVE
AND YOU CAN HOLD
DON'T BE WEAK
JUST BE BOLD
DON'T GIVE UP
DON'T GIVE IN
KEEP ON GOING
YOU CAN WIN
IT'S YOURS TO TAKE
YOURS TO KEEP
AND WHAT YOU SOW
YOU SO SHALL REAP

62. COULD IT BE MAGIC?

COULD IT BE MAGIC
THE STARS IN THE SKY
THE FLOWERS IN BLOOM
THE CLOUDS DRIFTING BY
THE TRICKLING WATER
THE WHISPERING BREEZE
THE BIRDS FLYING ROUND
AND LEAVES ON THE TREES.

COULD IT BE MAGIC
THE MOON OUT AT NIGHT
THE LAMBS IN A FIELD
THE SUN SHINING BRIGHT
THE BEES IN THE FLOWERS
THE BUTTERFLIES WINGS
THE VALLEYS AND HILLS
AND MANY MORE THINGS

COULD IT BE MAGIC
AND CAN IT BE TRUE
ALL THAT WE SEE
IS FOR ME AND FOR YOU
COULD IT BE MAGIC
IT HAPPENS TO BE
WONDERFUL SIGHTS
FOR YOU AND FOR ME.

63. THANK YOU...

THANK YOU FOR THE BRAND NEW DAY
THAT STARTED BRIGHT AND CLEAR
THANK YOU FOR THE SUN THAT SHINES
THAT BRINGS ME SO MUCH CHEER
I'M GRATEFUL FOR THE CHANCE TO HEAR
THE BIRDS THAT SING SO SWEET
AND SEE THEM IN MY GARDEN
IT REALLY IS A TREAT
THANK YOU FOR THE PLANTS THAT GROW
THEIR COLOURS NEW AND BRIGHT
THEIR SMELLS SO SWEET AND FRAGRANT
SUCH A PLEASANT SIGHT
I'M GRATEFUL FOR THE CHANCE TO SEE
ALL THE THINGS I SEE
TO HAVE THE THINGS AROUND I HAVE
AND HAVE THE CHANCE TO BE
THANK YOU FOR THE WORLD AROUND
IT'S SUCH A JOYOUS PLACE
OURS TO LOVE, OURS TO SHARE
IT ALWAYS WILL AMAZE
I'M GRATEFUL FOR THE CHANCE TO SAY
THANKS FOR EVERYTHING
IT PUTS A SMILE UPON MY FACE
AND MAKES MY POOR HEART SING

64. THAT'S LIFE!

OUT OF PLACE
AND NOT IN TIME
NOT IN RHYTHM
OUT OF RHYME
PULLING THIS WAY
PUSHING THAT
NOT QUITE KNOWING
WHERE YOU'RE AT.

MOVING FORWARD
FALLING BACK
LOSING GROUND
THEN BACK ON TRACK
GETTING UP
AND THEN YOU FALL
OUT OF LUCK
THEN HAVE IT ALL.

ASK THE QUESTION
NO REPLY
"WHAT IS LIFE?"
AND ALSO "WHY?"
DOES IT MATTER?
SHOULD WE CARE?
LIFE IS HERE
AND EVERYWHERE.

JUST BE HAPPY
JUST BE GLAD
FOR WHAT YOU HAVE
AND WHAT YOU'VE HAD
LIFE IS SHORT
SO FILL EACH DAY
AND DO YOUR BEST
IN YOUR OWN WAY.

65. SOMETIMES – I WONDER.

SOMETIMES I FEEL LIKE I'VE DONE WRONG
AND REALLY DON'T KNOW WHY
I FIND THAT ALL THAT I CAN DO
IS SIT AROUND AND CRY
SOMETIMES I FEEL SO LONELY
SO LOST AND ON MY OWN
I WONDER WHERE TO TURN TO
WHILE I AM ALL ALONE
SOMETIMES I FEEL LIKE I'VE GONE WRONG
AND NEED TO PUT THINGS RIGHT
BUT DON'T KNOW WHAT IT IS I'VE DONE
IT HAUNTS ME DAY AND NIGHT.
SOMETIMES I FEEL SO OUT OF PLACE
AND DON'T KNOW WHERE TO GO
I'LL SIT AROUND JUST WONDERING
AND WAIT UNTIL I KNOW
SOMETIMES I FEEL SO HAPPY
I CANNOT UNDERSTAND
WHY I HAVE THOSE OTHER THOUGHTS
THAT GET SO OUT OF HAND.

66. THAT'S ME!

JUST BECAUSE I SOMETIMES CRY
DOES NOT MEAN I'M WEAK
I'M STRONGER THAN YOU REALIZE
ALTHOUGH I MAY NOT SPEAK
I STAND UPON MY OWN TWO FEET
BUT SOMETIMES I FALL DOWN
BUT WHEN I'M DOWN I'LL GET BACK UP
AND WILL NOT WEAR A FROWN
THE SMILE I WEAR UPON MY FACE
WILL SOMETIMES HIDE MY PAIN
BUT MOSTLY IT IS JUST PURE JOY
THAT MAKES ME SMILE AGAIN
I'LL GO FOR WHAT I WANT IN LIFE
I NEVER WILL GIVE IN
I'LL KEEP ON PUSHING FORWARD
UNTIL AT LAST I WIN
I'LL GO FOR WHAT I THINK IS BEST
I'LL TRY AND NOT GIVE WAY
UNTIL I REACH MY FINAL GOAL
AND MAKE THE PERFECT DAY
AND THOUGH SOME PEOPLE THINK I'M WEAK
BELIEVE ME I AM STRONG
I'LL JUST KEEP MOVING FORWARD
TO WHERE I SHOULD BELONG
WITH YOU OR WITHOUT YOU
I KNOW THAT I CAN BE
A PERSON IN MY OWN WAY
I'LL SHOW YOU - WAIT AND SEE.

67. LOST IN SPACE?

I CANNOT SEE IN FRONT OF ME
I CANNOT SEE BEHIND
ALL AROUND IS GREY AND DULL
IT'S LIKE THE WORLD'S GONE BLIND
THE AIR IS STILL AND QUIET
NOTHING MOVES ABOUT
STANDING ON THIS COLD DARK DAY
MAKES ME WANT TO SHOUT
"IS ANYBODY OUT THERE?
IS ANYBODY NEAR?
IS ANYBODY LISTENING?
CAN ANYBODY HEAR?"
IT'S LIKE I MUST BE LOST IN SPACE
DRIFTING OUT OF VIEW
NOT SURE EVEN WHERE TO GO
AND NOT SURE WHAT TO DO
CAN ANYBODY SEE ME?
I WONDER ONCE AGAIN
I WISH WE DIDN'T HAVE THIS FOG
I'D RATHER HAVE THE RAIN!

68. THE BIRDS.

THE BIRDS THAT I FEED IN MY GARDEN
COME BACK TO ME DAY AFTER DAY
THEY EAT UP THE SEEDS AND THE NUTS I PUT DOWN
THEY'LL SIT AND THEY'LL SING WHEN THEY STAY
EACH OF THEM FEELS LIKE AN OLD FRIEND
THEY'RE WELCOME TO COME IN AND DINE
DON'T CARE IF THEY'RE PLAIN OR THEY'RE SIMPLE
EACH ONE IS A FRIEND WHO IS MINE.
THEY'RE TRUE AND THEY'RE FAITHFUL AND LOYAL
THEY WATCH AS I POTTER AROUND
THEY JOIN ME EACH DAY IN THE GARDEN
THEY SIT ON THE FENCE OR THE GROUND
AS SOON AS THEY SEE ME THEY SING OUT
I CALL BACK A CHEERFUL "HELLO"
I'M SURE THAT EACH ONE UNDERSTANDS ME
FOR THEY MAKE NO EFFORT TO GO
I LOVE EACH AND EVERY ONE OF THEM
THEY BRIGHTEN THE DULLEST OF DAY
I WELCOME THE BIRDS TO MY GARDEN
AND HOPE THAT THEY ALWAYS WILL STAY.

69. SUNSHINE AND SHOWERS

IF SUNSHINE AND SHOWERS
BRINGS FLOWERS TO BLOOM
IT ALSO BRINGS COLOURS
TO BRIGHTEN THE GLOOM
IT LIFTS SPIRITS HIGH
MAKING THEM SOAR
IT ALSO BRINGS HAPPINESS
VERY MUCH MORE
SMILES UPON FACES
TO BRIGHTEN A DAY
CHEERING YOU UP
AS YOU GO ON YOUR WAY
MAY SUNSHINE AND SHOWERS
KEEP WORKING THEIR THING
CHANGING THE DAY
WITH WHAT THEY CAN BRING

70. A NEW DAY

FREE AS THE WIND
MY SPIRIT CAN SOAR
NOT BLOCKED BY A WINDOW
STOPPED BY A DOOR
OVER THE VALLEYS
THE HILLS AND THE DALES
MY SPIRIT FLIES FREE
WITH A BREEZE IN ITS SAILS
OVER THE GREEN FIELDS
DOWN BY A STREAM
ALL THROUGH THE TREES
JUST LIKE IN A DREAM
THE SUN SHINING BRIGHT
NO CLOUDS IN THE SKY
JUST WATCHING SLOWLY
TIME PASSING BY
THE DAY IS MY OWN
BRIGHT SHINING AND NEW
I LET MY MIND FREE
WITH NOTHING TO DO

71. CONVERSATION PIECE

HALF HEARD CONVERSATIONS
YOU HEAR WHILST YOU'RE ABOUT
THINGS THAT NEEDED DOING
THERE'S SOMEONE HAS A DOUBT
THERE'S CLEANING THAT NEEDS DOING
SOME GRASS THAT'S NEEDED MOWN
AND SOMEONE HAS A PHOTOGRAPH
WANTING TO BE SHOWN
SOMEONE'S GOING WALKING
THERE'S SHOPPING TO BE DONE
SOMEONE SPENT THEIR YESTERDAY
SITTING IN THE SUN
THE TV WAS QUITE BORING
FOR SOMEONE ELSE LAST NIGHT
CAKES THAT NEEDED BAKING
SOME SHOES ARE FAR TOO TIGHT
THESE HALF HEARD CONVERSATIONS
THE FRAGMENTS THAT YOU HEAR
CAN ALL BE QUITE AMUSING
WHEN COMING TO THE EAR!

72. STRANGERS ON A TRAIN

I DON'T KNOW WHERE SHE'S FROM
I DIDN'T ASK HER NAME
WE SAT TOGETHER SIDE BY SIDE
OUR STORIES MUCH THE SAME
OUR JOURNEY WASN'T VERY LONG
OUR STORIES STARTED SMALL
BUT AS THE STATIONS PASSED US BY
WE TOLD EACH OTHER ALL
THE ROADS THAT WE BOTH TRAVELLED
WERE NOT THAT FAR APART
THE STORIES THAT WE BOTH TOLD
WERE COMING FROM THE HEART
TWO HEARTS THAT HAD BEEN BROKEN
FOUR EYES HAD CRIED IN PAIN
WE PARTED AT OUR JOURNEYS END
TO NEVER MEET AGAIN

73. IN LIFE

THEY SAY THAT FOOLS ARE LONELY
AND SAY THE LONELY CRY
I'VE DONE MY SHARE OF CRYING
THE LONELY FOOL IS I
THERE'S NONE SO BLIND THAT CANNOT SEE
WITH NO DIRECTION TOO
AND STUMBLE BLINDLY ON AND ON
NOT KNOWING WHAT TO DO
AND LIKE A FOOL I'M THINKING
THAT ALL WILL BE ALRIGHT
BLINDED BY THE TEARS THAT FALL
EVERY DAY AND NIGHT
AND SOMEHOW IN MY FOOLISHNESS
I JUST KEEP GOING ON
I REALISE I AM NOT THE FOOL
AND NOT THE ONLY ONE.

74. I AM WHAT I AM

A VOYAGE OF DISCOVERY
A JOURNEY MADE THROUGH TIME
THE TRAVELS THAT I MAKE IN LIFE
WILL NEVER BE SUBLIME
EXCITEMENT FROM ADVENTURES
ON PATHS I TRAVEL ON
THE CHOICES THAT I MAKE IN LIFE
BEFORE MY LIFE IS GONE
ALL ALONE OR WITH SOMEONE
THE JOURNEY THAT I MAKE
IS MINE AND MINE ALONE
WHATEVER PATH I TAKE
TO MAKE OF LIFE WHATEVER
AND DO THE BEST I CAN
I STARTED IN MY CHILDHOOD
I DO IT AS A MAN
I AM THE MAN I AM NOW
FROM CHOICES THAT I TOOK
I CANNOT CHANGE MY HISTORY
A SLOWLY CLOSING BOOK
I CARRY ON CREATING
I LIKE THE MAN I SEE
DOING ALL THE THINGS I DO
THE MAN I SEE IS ME

75. ...I NEVER THOUGHT I WOULD AGAIN...

OUT AND ABOUT AND LOOKING ROUND
YOU'D NEVER GUESS WHAT I'D JUST FOUND
I COULDN'T BELIEVE WHAT I HAD SEEN
WHAT IT WAS, WHAT MIGHT HAVE BEEN
I HADN'T SEEN ONE FOR SOME TIME
SO IMPRESSED I WROTE THIS RHYME
IF YOU HAD SEEN WHAT I HAD SEEN
YOU'D THINK YOU'D STEPPED IN TO A DREAM
I NEVER THOUGHT THAT THERE COULD BE
A SIGHT LIKE THAT FOR US TO SEE
YOU DO NOT SEE ONE EVERY DAY
OR EVEN SEE ONE IN THIS WAY
THE BIGGEST ONE THAT I HAVE KNOWN
STARTED SMALL AND SOON HAD GROWN
OH SO BEAUTIFUL AND BRIGHT
WHAT A JOY AND WHAT A SIGHT
THIS ONE WAS THE BEST ONE YET
A MOST INCREDIBLE SUNSET.

www.ingramcontent.com/pod-product-compliance
Lightning Source LLC
LaVergne TN
LVHW021135080426
835509LV00010B/1360